*For my own mother (and greatest fan and strongest critic), Yvonne Epstein, for more reasons than I can list here. With much love.*

# GOOD CLEAN FUN

**Cynthia MacGregor**

Robins Lane Press
a division of Gryphon House, Inc.

www.robinslane.com

**Library of Congress Cataloging-in-Publication Data**

MacGregor, Cynthia.
    Good Clean Fun / Cynthia MacGregor.
        p.    cm.
  Includes index
  ISBN 158904-003-1
  1. Games.   I. Title.
GV1203.M319   2001

                  2001023725

Published by Robins Lane Press
A division of Gryphon House
10726 Tucker St., Beltsville, MD 20705 U.S.A.
Printed in the United States of America
International Standard Book Number: 158904-003-1
01  02  03  04  05  06     15  14  13  12  11  10  9  8  7  6  5  4  3  2  1

# Contents

# Acknowledgments

As always, thanks to Vic Bobb.
Thanks also to Lenna Buissink.

# Imagination Stretchers

2 or more players

Encourage your children to let their creativity run free with this activity.

Ask the players a question, such as, "What's a good use for a cardboard box?" Encourage the players to respond with a silly answer (the wilder and sillier, the better). For example, "Fill it with water and go swimming in it." "Put a propeller on it and fly it to Grandma's." "Paint it purple, stick a feather in it, and wear it as a hat."

This is not a game with scoring, so there is no "wrong" answer. While sensible responses are perfectly all right, wild answers are even better.

Who knows—you may be harboring a budding inventor in your house!

# Impromptu Jigsaw Puzzles

2 or more players
*Materials needed: Pens or crayons and paper*

This activity works best with more than one child, because the premise is for each child to create a puzzle, then give it to another child to solve.

Give each child a piece of paper and pens or crayons to draw a picture (the more complex the better). Remind the children not to leave any large areas blank.

When the children finish drawing their pictures, each child tears his picture into a number of pieces (four or five for younger children, as many as sixteen or more for older ones). When all the puzzles are torn into pieces, the children trade puzzles and try to put each other's puzzles back together.

The purpose of these puzzles is to entertain children during a waiting period. It is unfair to reward the first child to reassemble a puzzle because the puzzles will vary in complexity. For example, one child's puzzle might be considerably more complicated than another's, or there might be a great difference in ages.

These impromptu jigsaw puzzles may not endure for years of play, but they don't need to! Their purpose is to entertain during a waiting period, and for that they'll do fine.

# Stare-Down

2 players

This game is deceptively simple. The object is to see which player can stare the longest at the other without blinking. The first player to blink or look away loses.

Neither player is allowed to speak or make any noises.

## Variations

When you think you've mastered Blinking 101, make fierce or silly faces to try and get your opponent look away, giggle or blink.

# Floor Tile Counting

2 or more players

This activity may sound a bit mundane, but for younger children, it can be a fun way to pass the time while waiting in an airport, train station or doctor's office.

Challenge your child to count floor tiles. For example, "Hey! Let's see if you can count the floor tiles along the wall from here to the newspaper vending machine" (or ". . . from the water fountain to that gate," ". . . from the payphone to the Ladies' Room," and so on). Make sure not to pick a destination that will take a small child out of your sight; how far you let the child wander should be in direct proportion to his age.

You will be surprised at the number of opportunities that exist for such an activity in an airport, train station, bus terminal or other places—all without letting your young one out of your sight.

In a situation where the floor is carpeted, ask the child to count the ceiling tiles. Or ask her to count the number of steps it takes to walk from where you are sitting to a given spot in the terminal.

# Rhyme Game

2 or more players

Kids love rhyming. Give your children a challenge: ask them how many rhymes they can think of for various words that you tell them. For example, "How many words can you think of that rhyme with 'list'?"

## Variations

Keep a list of the words the kids say. The children can later try to use these words to make up poems. It doesn't matter if the poem sounds choppy, the meter's off, or it doesn't scan right. The object is to get your child to play with language and be creative.

# Powers Of Observation

2 or more players

Just how observant are your children? Find out by playing this fun game.

Ask the players to close and cover their eyes (no peeking!) and describe their surroundings as accurately as they can. If you're in the family car, for example, that faithful vehicle in which they've ridden so often, they should be able to describe it pretty accurately. But can they? Ask them for as many details as they can provide. Then, when they finish with what they remember about the car, ask questions about any items they've failed to describe. For example, ask them what you or other occupants of the car are wearing today.

If you run out of details to inquire about in your present surroundings, quiz the children about

8

details back home. For example, "Do you know exactly how many trees are in the backyard?" "Do you remember how many cabinets are in the kitchen?" "What color are the towels in the hall bathroom?"

# Hopping Race

2 or more players

Turn a deserted, or semi-deserted concourse into an impromptu racecourse with this activity!

Challenge your child to hop on one foot from where you're standing to a suitable marker down the hall (for example, a water fountain or payphone), then to hop back on the other foot. If you have two or more children with you, they can make it a race. If you only have one child with you, he can race against the clock.

## Variations

Encourage other forms of locomotion, such as walking sideways. Walking backward is not recommended, as it could cause the child to bump into other pedestrians.

# Magazine Tales

2 players
*Materials needed: Old magazines*

Open a magazine and ask your child to find a picture that she finds interesting. (It's fine for the picture to be part of an ad.)

Ask her to make up a story about the people in the picture. If she is slow to get started, prompt her with a few questions: "What do you suppose they were doing right before the picture was taken?" "How do you suppose the people in the picture might be related to each other—or are they just friends, or even strangers?" "What might they be about to do next?" "What are their names?"

This game is more fun if you play without the pressure to come up with a perfect story, complete with beginning, middle and end.

# Find The Letters

2 players
*Materials needed: Old magazines*

This is a good activity if you're filling time in a doctor's waiting room with a child who's just learning his alphabet.

Open one of the magazines on the table and ask the child to find all the letter "As" that he can. Continue with the letter "B," "C," "D" and so on. Keep in mind that different magazines use different typefaces; therefore, an "a" (lower case) or even an "A" (capital) may look quite different from one magazine to the next. Try to find a magazine with a simple typeface, so your child will have the least difficulty recognizing the letters. The more familiar their form, the easier his search.

If the child grows tired of searching for random letters, ask him to find all the letters that make up his name.

# Highway To The Past

2 or more players

As you and your children ride along a road (whether it's an interstate, country road or an urban street), the children look out the window and call out an object they see (for example, pigeon, barn, barbershop, stop sign and so on). You must then supply a story about your own past or your family's history involving that object (not that specific barbershop, pigeon, or barn of course).

For example, you could tell the story of how you and your brother went to Uncle Mort's farm one summer and played ball against the side of the barn. Or, you might tell about the first time you took the child who said, "Barbershop" for his first haircut. (Kids love hearing stories about themselves.)

# Memory and Knowledge Challenge

2 or more players

Pick any subject that you and the players are knowledgeable about. Start asking the children questions, such as "Name the 50 states." "What's the capital of Rhode Island?" "How many presidents of the U.S. can you name?" "How many world leaders can you name?" "What are three examples of an adjective?"

Even young children can answer questions. For example, "What are the names of the two streets at either end of our block?" "What streets do we cross to get to Bobby's house?" "Name three kinds of trees." "How many flowers can you name?"

You don't need to reward correct answers. Children love to show off, and they will be happy just to shout out the answers. (If they don't know answers they should know, you will now know what subjects they need to brush up on at home!)

# If You Were _____

2 or more players

In addition to Fanta-Tease (page 33), another thought-provoking kind of question to ask your children to occupy some time is the "What would you do if you were _____?" or "What would your life be like if you were _____?" type of question.

Some examples of these kinds of questions are:

- What would you do if you were President of the United States?
- What laws would you make if you were this state's governor?
- What would you do for fun if you were a famous rock star?
- What charities would you give some of your money to if you were rich?

- If you had a million dollars you could use to improve the world, how would you spend it?
- If you were president of a large corporation, and you had an idea that would make lots of money for the company but would harm the earth's environment, what would you do?
- If you were running for class president, and one of your friends knew something bad about the person who was running against you, would you use that information in your campaign?

Don't feel limited to these questions—dream up some of your own. Also, feel free to change these questions if you think your children will relate better to an alternative form of a question.

# I Have a Big Head

2 or more players

One player starts by saying, "I have a big head," while pointing to any other part of her body but her head (for example, her elbow). The next player repeats, "I have a big head," while pointing to her own elbow. She also adds a similar description, such as "and blue eyes," while pointing to any part of her body but her eyes (for example, her foot).

The next player says, "I have a big head (while pointing to her elbow) and blue eyes (while pointing to her foot)." She adds another description and points to a different part of her body.

The game continues as players repeat the previous descriptions while pointing to the correct body parts. The players also add a new description and point to a new body part each turn. The players must correctly repeat both the spoken words and the purposely false pointing. Any player who makes a mistake is out of the game, and the last one left wins the game.

# After "Happily Ever After"

2 or more players

A fun kind of storytelling is to pick up the thread of a famous story after the established ending.

For example, what happened to Cinderella after Prince Charming discovered that the slipper fit and they got married? Did she eventually become Queen? Did she have children? How many, and what were their names?

Or, what happened to the Three Little Pigs after the Big Bad Wolf failed to blow down the practical pig's brick house? Did he go away mad and stay away, or did he devise a scheme to come back and try again? What was his plan? Did it work? If not, how did the pigs foil him?

## Variations

Write down the story as the children tell it. You can even encourage the children to act it out. Who knows—you may find you have a budding actor in your family!

# Survey Says

2 or more players

This is a good activity if you and your child are in a clearly defined small area within a larger terminal (for example, the waiting area of a gate at an airport). If you feel that your child can walk around the area safely, ask her to count the total number of people sitting in the area. For example, tell your child, "I wonder how many other people are waiting for this same plane? Why don't you count all the people sitting in this little area from over there to over there?"

## Variations

If you have a younger child or if you are in an area where you don't want your child to wander away, ask her to count the number of people who walk by in three minutes. You can watch the time while your child counts.

Another possibility is to let your child stand on one of the seats or benches—a delicious possibility for her, as standing on furniture is probably a no-no at home—and count something, such as the number of bald-headed men she sees, or the number of people wearing hats. (Be sure to caution her not to count aloud, "One bald man, two bald men"!) This activity, besides being a time-passer, also sharpens your child's observation skills.

# Progressive Stories

2 or more players

Progressive Stories are fun and a challenge to the imagination, especially when one player sticks another player with the responsibility of picking up the story at a "cliffhanger" point. Parental participation isn't required, but play along if you want to join the fun.

Decide the order in which you'll proceed. The first player begins to tell a tale (realistic or unbelievable). She might choose to set the story in the present, or it could be a futuristic yarn set in outer space or a story of the pioneers in the Old West.

A couple of minutes into her story, she stops and turns the story over to the next player. It is best (but not necessary) if a player turns the story over to the next player at a crucial point (for example, when the heroine is trapped in a time tunnel or facing a stampeding herd of cattle). The player can turn the story over to the next player with a dramatic statement, such as, "He couldn't believe his eyes when he turned the corner and saw. . . ."

As the players take turns, the setting and plot of the story is likely to change wildly, and a story that started out on the moon could wind up in your neighbor's back yard. It doesn't matter if the story defies all literary conventions, as long as the children are having a good time.

The game is over when the story has come to a logical ending, or when the players get bored and want to try something else. If they're tired of Johnny and his seemingly unending story, for example, they can leave him floating in space or facing those alligators!

**Hint**

If the children are slow to get started with Progressive Stories, you can always lend a hand by starting the first story yourself. Quickly bring the story to a cliffhanger point and then turn it over to the next player. Away they'll go!

# Silence!

2 or more players

The rule for this game is as simple as the rules for "Stare-Down" (page 4): Players must be silent. Talking, giggling and toe tapping are not allowed.

You can play that the first player to make a noise loses. Or, you can play a cumulative scoring game by giving each player who makes a noise one point. The first player to score ten points loses.

Enjoy the silence while it lasts!

## Variations

Make a rule that children are allowed to make faces to try to get each other to giggle or talk. Or, make keeping a straight face part of the rules (to keep the children even more decorous).

# Street Sign Name Game

1 or more players

The only requirement for this car travel game is that children are old enough to spell their names and recognize the letters of the alphabet.

The challenge of this game is for players to spell their names using the letters they spot on passing signs. For example, if a player's name is Alicia, her challenge is to scan the signs that you pass and search, in order, for an "A," "L," "I," and so on. If you are driving on a highway, she can scan mileage signs, exit signs and billboards. In town, she can check store name signs, window signs and street signs.

If there are three kids in the car, they can all try to spell their own names, but don't turn it into a contest to see who can spell his name first. For example, it's unfair to have Alexander or Theodore competing with Matt or Don. Poor Alexander has the double burden of a long name and one with a difficult-to-find letter in it.

## Variations

If the children enjoy the game but spell their names too quickly, encourage them to spell their friends' names, a pet's name or familiar words such as "ICE CREAM" or "BREAKFAST."

# Crambo

3 or more players (the more, the better)

Select one player to be the leader and ask her to think of a secret word. Once she has thought of her word, she gives a clue to the other players by saying a word that rhymes with her chosen word. For example, if her secret word is "shed," she tells the other players that she is thinking of a word that rhymes with "head."

Using the rhyme the leader has given, the other players must guess the word by asking leading questions. In this instance, the first player might ask, "Is it something you make a sandwich with?" The leader must figure out what word the player is thinking of and then answer, "No, it's not 'bread.'"

If a player stumps the leader with his question, he must tell the leader the word he was thinking of.

The player then gets to ask another question. Play continues until one player guesses correctly. That player becomes the new leader, thinks of a new word and starts another round.

# Fanta-Tease

1 or more players

This is a good way to involve your children in creative thought when they have time on their hands.

Pose hypothetical questions that make the children think creatively. Because this isn't literally a game, there is no maximum or minimum number of players required. Here are some questions you can ask:

- If a foreign exchange student came to stay in your house, where would you take him that would show him America as you know it?
- What would you do if you had x-ray vision?
- Suppose you were allowed to meet with the President of the United States. What would you want to tell the President?

- Suppose you could make the laws. What new laws would you pass? Locally? For the nation?
- If you suddenly were invisible, how would you take advantage of that condition? What would be bad about it?
- If the human body could be redesigned, how would you do it?
- If you could wave a magic wand and create a new animal, what would it be? What would you call it? What noise would it make?
- If a genie popped out of a bottle and granted you three wishes, what would you wish for? If you weren't allowed to wish for anything for yourself, what would your three wishes be?
- If you were in charge of your school, what changes would you make?

- If you could "order up" a best friend, what would she be like?
- If you could be any animal, what animal would you be?
- What are your favorite things in life?
- What do you think most needs to be changed about the world?

These questions are just to get you started. Ask the children any questions you want and encourage them to ask you questions, too.

# Fake Commercials

2 or more players

Children love to play that they're on TV or the radio. So, challenge them to write a fake commercial.

The average child is exposed to enough commercials that she should be familiar with the genre. If your children have never thought about what constitutes a commercial, give them a brief explanation. Explain that a commercial is a message designed to sell a product and to make viewers or listeners run right out and buy "Barf-O, the Miracle Cereal," or "Goldie Goodies Goldfish Food."

The children don't necessarily have to script out the commercial. Some children will want to write it down, work it out and meticulously hone their presentation. (These children may have a future in the advertising business!) Others, though, will prefer to deliver their commercials on the spot, making it up as they go. Younger children may have to deliver a spoken commercial that hasn't been written down, unless they dictate it to an adult or older child first.

When the children are through with the activity, take a serious moment to ask if they understand the purpose of commercials. If the children comprehend the motivation behind commercials, the next time someone on TV tells them they must have a certain toy, they may be a tad less vulnerable to the pitch.

Hopefully, you've not only staved off twenty minutes of boredom, you've also instilled a tiny bit of immunity into your junior consumers!

# Spontaneous Math

2 players

Encourage your children to do real world math problems based on the objects around them. (This activity also sharpens their math skills without using a pencil and paper.)

The difficulty level of the problems (and whether they involve only addition and subtraction or also multiplication and division) depends on the child's age and math skills.

The problems you pose can be as simple as, "There are five chairs on that side of the room and two on this side. If we took one of those chairs and put it over here, how many chairs would be on this side?" or "If there are two men, three women and a child in the waiting room, how many people are there altogether?" or "If there are five people in the waiting room and two go inside, how many are left?"

They can also be more complicated, such as "If the doctor spends fifteen minutes with each patient and there are five patients in the waiting room, how long will it take him to see all of his patients if no one else shows up?" Or, "Let's say there are five people in the waiting room, but two of them are just waiting with other people. There is one person in with the doctor now and six more people are going to show up during the afternoon. How many people will the doctor see all afternoon?"

# Progressive Plates

1 or more players

This in-the-car game is best played cooperatively. It's as much fun for four or more players as it is for one.

The rules are easy: Count the numbers on the license plates of passing cars. Start at the number one and count up (two, three, four and so on) to whatever number you desire. After the players get through the single-digit numbers, look for 10, 11, 12, and so on, making sure that the digits are together. For example, there is an 11 in 9112, but not in 9121.

## Variations

If this game is too easy for your children and it ends too quickly, try playing "Double Digits" instead. The principle is the same—the players cooperatively hunt for license plate numbers in progression. However, instead of looking for the numbers one through 21 in order, they are on the lookout for the double numbers 00 through 99 in order (for example, 00, 11, 22 and so on).

# I'm Going Shopping

2 or more players

This game of memory and repetition works for two players as well as a lot of players. It's extremely well suited for car travel.

One player begins by saying, "I'm going shopping and I'm buying ____." She fills in the blank with any item that begins with "A," such as "apples." The next player repeats the first player's statement, adding a "B" item as well. For example, "I'm going shopping and I'm buying apples and a bicycle." The next player repeats the second player's phrase and adds an item beginning with the letter "C" and so on.

If a player is unable to think of an item in time, or incorrectly recalls a previous player's item, she is out of the game. In a two-player game, when one player is eliminated, the other player is automatically the winner. When there are three or more players, when one player is eliminated, the other players continue until only one player is left. The last player remaining is the winner.

# Coffeepot

2 or more players

Do you coffeepot? That depends on what "coffeepot" is, and guessing correctly is the challenge of this game.

Choose one player to be "It" and ask her to leave the room (or cover her ears). The other players agree on a common verb, such as brushing (teeth), walking, bathing or whistling. They will replace the chosen verb with the word "coffeepot."

When the players have chosen a verb, bring It back into the room. It can ask twenty questions to try to figure out what "coffeepot" is. She can ask questions such as, "Do you coffeepot at home?" or "Do you coffeepot everyday?"

When she thinks she knows what it is, she can ask, "Is 'coffeepot' dusting?" If she guesses correctly, she wins! If she guesses incorrectly, there is no penalty and she can continue asking questions (up to twenty). However, each guess counts as a question. If she uses all twenty questions and cannot figure out what "coffeepot" is, she loses.

## Variations

For a younger group of players, allow It to ask as many questions as she needs to guess the verb in question. If she guesses the correct verb, she wins. If she gives up, she loses.

Instead of playing by the twenty-question rule, let each player have a turn being It and let her ask as many questions as desired. However, the player who guesses what "coffeepot" is by asking the fewest number of questions is the winner.

# I Spy

2 or more players

Choose one player to be the leader. The leader selects anything within his sight to be the "secret object." He does not tell the other players what object he has chosen, but says, "I spy with my eye something that begins with the letter ____," adding the letter with which the object begins.

The other players take turns guessing (in order) what the secret object is. They cannot ask about the object's qualities or location, such as "Is it high?" "Is it blue?" "Is it in the room or outside?" Instead, they may only ask direct guesses. For example, "Is it a book?" "Is it the bookcase?" "Is it the bug on the window?"

If there are only two players, you can set a limit on the number of guesses allowed per round. In addition, you can keep track of how many guesses each player uses to correctly identify the secret object, and name the winner by who needed fewer guesses.

# I Want To Sell You A Kangaroo

2 or more players

To begin this game, one player faces another and names an object, such as a kangaroo. The second player must give a brief speech about the object. For example, she might say, "I want to sell you a kangaroo. You really should buy it because . . ." The player then gives as many reasons as she can think of that the first player should buy the kangaroo (or whatever the object is).

The second player's reasons do not need to be sensible. In fact, the more outrageous they are, the more fun the game is! Some reasons for buying a kangaroo might include, "If you miss the school bus, you could ride to school in its pocket," and "On a cold day, the pocket would be a good place to keep warm."

# Cause And Effect

3 players

This game isn't played for points or for winners—
it's played just for silly fun!

The first player makes a simple statement. The
second player gives a cause for the first player's
statement. The third player provides an effect, or
result, of the second player's statement. The only
requirements are that the second and third players' answers MUST BE SILLY.

For example, the first player makes a simple
statement, such as "I missed the school bus today."
The second player provides a silly cause. For example, "Because I was building a bear trap on the roof
and didn't come down in time." The last player
gives a silly effect, such as, "So I had to grow wings
and fly to school."

That's the end of a round! For the next round, change the order in which everyone speaks so that everyone gets to supply a different part. Play until everyone has had enough or when everybody is laughing so hard, you need to take a break and play something else!

# Applaud The Truth

3 or more players

This isn't a good game to play in a quiet public place because it involves loud applause.

Choose one person to be the leader. She makes a simple statement, which is immediately identifiable as either true or false. As soon as she says the statement, she applauds. If what she says is true, the other players should immediately join in the applause.

If, however, it is a false statement, the other players should not clap. Any player who applauds to a false statement, or fails to clap immediately for a true statement, is out of the game. Players must respond quickly! If they hesitate, they're out.

When only one player (besides the leader) is left, she is declared the winner and is the leader for the next round.

This game is much more fun with a lot of players. In a three-player game, as soon as one player is out, the other is the winner already (the third player is the leader) and the game is over.

# All Birds Fly

2 or more players

Choose one player to be the leader. The leader says, "All birds fly," and makes flapping motions with his arms. (If you are playing this in a car, the leader can make flapping motions with his hands instead.) The leader then names things that may or may not fly. Every time he names something, he will make flapping motions with his arms. The leader mentions some things that really fly, such as robins, beetles, sparrows and hawks. However, he can also toss in things that don't fly, such as horses, buildings and other absurdities.

The other players must flap along with the leader when he mentions things that fly and refrain from flapping when he mentions things that don't. Any players who fail to flap on an appropriate noun, or who flap on an inappropriate noun, are out of the game. The last one left wins the game. Players take turns being the leader. Each leader chooses a different verb to replace "fly."

# Ghost

2 players

With this game, you don't have to wait until Halloween to be a ghost! However, if you become a GHOST, you're out of the game.

Play begins with the first player saying any letter of the alphabet. If he says "H," for example, the second player must think of a word that begins with "H". If he thinks of the word "HOUSE," for example, he would give the second letter of the word—in this case, "O."

The first player thinks of a word that begins with "HO." He will then say the third letter of the word. For example, if he thinks of "HOME," he would say "M." The player must be careful not to choose a letter that completes a word, though.

If a player cannot think of a word that is spelled with the combination of letters he has been given, he would then challenge the other player. If the other player can spell a word with the letters, the challenger loses the round. If the other player is bluffing and cannot spell a word, he loses the round. Play continues until one player completes the spelling of a word or if a player successfully challenges another player.

Every time a player loses a round of the game, he gets a letter of the word "GHOST." The player would first get a "G," then an "H," then an "O,"and so on. The first player to get to G-H-O-S-T loses.

# ABC Objects

2 or more players

The players take turns challenging another player by saying any letter of the alphabet (except "Q," "U," "V," "W," "X," "Y" and "Z," which are unfairly difficult for this game). She counts to five slowly ("One thousand and one, one thousand and two" and so on).

Within that time frame, the challenged player must name an object that begins with that letter. The object must be a thing—not a person or place—and it must be an everyday object.

If the challenged player fails to think of an object, or if he repeats a noun that was used earlier in the game, he is out of the game. The game continues until only one player is left, who is then declared the winner.

# Beep!

2 or more players

This game is similar to the numbers game "Buzz" (page 131), only it is a spelling game.

In this game, players spell words aloud and substitute the word "Beep!" for all vowels. For example, if the word is "READER," the player says, "R, Beep!, Beep!, D, Beep!, R."

If you are playing this game with one child, you pick the words to challenge your child. If he can spell five words correctly in a row, he wins. If two or more children are playing, they can come up with their own words to challenge each other. They can give each other five words, ten words or however many they have the time or patience for. The winner is the child who spells the most words correctly according to the rules of the game.

Spelling counts, by the way! If a player makes a mistake other than failing to say, "Beep!" for a vowel, that mistake counts against her. The player must spell the word correctly and say, "Beep!" for each vowel.

# Draw a Whazit

3 players
*Materials needed: Pen and paper*

Fold a piece of paper into thirds and unfold it. Choose one player to go first. To begin the game, he draws a head and neck on the top third of the piece of paper, without letting any of the other players see it. The head and neck may be of a person, an animal or an imaginary creature such as a space alien.

When the first player has finished drawing the head and neck, he continues drawing the neck a bit past the top fold of the paper, so that the second player will know where to continue drawing the picture. Then he folds the top third back (so the second player can't see what he's drawn) and passes the paper to the next player.

The second player draws the midsection of person, animal or imaginary creature. When he is finished, he draws slightly past the second fold to show the third player where to draw the legs and feet. He passes the paper to the third player after folding the paper back again, so that only the bottom third is showing. The third player finishes the picture by drawing legs and feet (two, four or even ten!).

When the third player finishes, the children can unfold the picture for all to behold. Surprise! A Whatzit!

# Word Lightning

2 players
*Materials needed: Watch with a second hand*

Choose one player to go first. The first player tells the second player a letter. The second player has sixty seconds to think of all the words that begin with that letter.

Here is an example: Rosa and Matt are playing against each other. Rosa tells Matt the letter "B." She then looks at her watch, and begins timing sixty seconds. Matt has a minute in which to write down as many words beginning with "B" that he can. For example, book, ball, bring, bill, bell, belly, button and so on until Rosa calls, "Time!"

After the first player calls "Time," the second player gives a letter to the first player. The first player thinks of as many words beginning with that letter as she can. Whoever thinks of the most words, wins.

In the name of fairness, the letters "Q," "U," "V," "W," "X," "Y" and "Z" should not be used.

## Variations

If more than two children are playing, they can take turns picking the letters, while the other players race to come up with the most words.

# Initials

2 or more players

Choose one person to be the leader. The leader asks the other players any questions he desires, such as, "What's your favorite food?" The other players must give answers that begin with their initials. For example, Cathy Robins' answer might be "Cooked Rice." (Answers need not be truthful or make sense.)

Give each player five seconds (ten for younger children) to come up with a suitable response. A player is "out" if he:

- Fails to reply within the given time frame,
- Replies with an answer that does not begin with his initials,
- Gives an answer that has already been used.

The last player left is the winner. The winner becomes the leader and the game continues.

# Mom's Eating Alligators!

1 or more players

This is a great game to play on long car trips! One of my friends started playing this game in his childhood, when he noticed that the letters on the license plate of a car in front of his were CYM. He immediately interpreted this as standing for "Cover Your Mouth." His sister, spotting another plate with the letters MEA on it, added, "Mom's Eating Alligators!" A game was born!

Encourage your children to put their brains to work. Ask them to make the funniest, silliest, craziest, goofiest slogans or sayings they can from the letter combinations they see on plates for the next few miles. However long the game lasts, you'll be that much closer to your destination!

# I'm Thinking Of Something

2 or more players

This simpler version of Twenty Questions is great for younger children. Choose one player to be the leader. The leader thinks of an object. He then tells the other players, "I'm thinking of something and it starts with ____," filling in the blank with the first letter of the object.

The other players ask yes-or-no questions about the secret object. However, they cannot ask open-ended questions, such as, "What color is it?" or "How large is it?"

Unlike Twenty Questions (page 88), there is no limit to the number of questions the players can ask. The players can continue until they guess the object or until they give up. If the players begin getting discouraged, give them additional hints, if desired.

For very young children, or with more difficult objects to guess, you can give additional clues, such as "I'm thinking of an animal and it starts with 'G'."

When playing with a small child, or when playing for the first time, pick an easy object. Choose a concrete object instead of an abstract idea, pick a familiar object and make it easy by choosing a general object instead of a specific object (for example, a ball rather than a baseball).

When playing with older players, add the rule that if a player guesses incorrectly, he is out of the game.

# "Top Ten" Lists

2 or more players
*Materials needed: Pen and paper*

Borrow a trick from David Letterman—encourage your children to make their own Top Ten lists. For example, they can think up the "Top Ten Reasons To Eat Lima Beans" or "Top Ten Excuses For Not Doing Your Homework." Both lists have comic potential in the right hands. Suggest that they come up with their own topics and make lists.

When they're finished, read them aloud from ten to one, à la Letterman himself!

# Boxes

*2 players*
*Materials needed: Pens and paper (graph paper is best, but any will do)*

Start by creating a grid of 100 dots, making rows of ten across and ten down. The players take turns drawing lines connecting two adjacent dots (horizontally or vertically, not diagonally). The object is to draw the fourth line to create a fully fenced-in box, while trying not to leave an opening for another player to make a box.

When a player creates a box by drawing the fourth line, she puts her initials inside the box. If a player draws one line, but manages to create two boxes, she claims both boxes with her initials. A player who successfully draws a box goes again; otherwise, play proceeds from player to player in turn, with each player drawing one line at a time.

Note that a player can draw a line wherever she wants—it may adjoin an existing line, but it doesn't have to. She can draw it in a far corner, nowhere near any other lines, if desired.

The game is over when the players have connected all the dots and every possible box has been enclosed. Tally up the number of boxes claimed by each player, according to initials. The player with the most boxes is the winner.

# Oprah's On!

2 or more players

This activity can take several forms. The child can
pretend to be Oprah, Ricki, Geraldo or another talk
show host, and mimic that personality's on-camera
manner.

The child can interview her "guests" (including you and anyone else who's with you). For example, if your carpool of restless wiggle worms is
comprised of your 12-year-old son and his friend,
one can interview the other on a subject close to
every schoolchild's heart, such as, "Do you believe
teachers today give too much homework?" Or they
can discuss serious issues, such as, "Is there a lot of
cheating going on in schools today? What's the
cause? What can be done about it?"

Turn the tables—you be Regis or Oprah and inter-view your child. Pretend she's a rock star or actor and ask her appropriate questions. She will have fun pretending that she's a famous and rich per-sonality.

The children can even make up funny com-mercials to break in with from time to time, if they want.

# Magazine Picture Scavenger Hunt

2 or more players
*Materials needed: Pens and paper, magazines*

Prepare a list of ten items that are likely to be pictured in magazines (including the ads). Give each player a copy of the list, and ask him to start thumbing through the magazines, looking for pictures of the items in question. For example, if you're going to be in a doctor's office with its usual assortment of magazines, you might include: a pen, car, dog, house, desk, computer, stove, football, sailboat and golf club.

Give the players a pen and paper so they can write down the magazine title and page numbers of each item they've found. The first player to complete his list is the winner. If no one can complete the list, the one who has found the most items after a suitable period is declared the winner.

## Variation

Instead of searching for objects, play Alphabet Magazine Scavenger Hunt. Ask your children to search for pictures of objects that begin with every letter of the alphabet. The first player to get to "Z" wins!

# Who Are They?

2 or more players

This is a good activity when you and your child are in a waiting area.

Discreetly single out any other person in the waiting area and ask your child, "What do you suppose that man does for a living?" "What do you suppose that woman does for fun?" "How old do you suppose that person is?"

Ask some questions that require factual guesses and some that require purely imaginary guesses. For example, if you ask your child to guess someone's age, she can make a straightforward guess by the person's appearance. Other questions may lead to answers that are pure imagination. For example, if your child decides that the man in the ill-fitting blue sports coat and brown pants must be a teacher "because he dresses funny, just like my teacher," you can't fault the reasoning!

In addition to asking your child to make guesses about specific people, such as their occupations, what kind of people they are or any other information your child might be able to guess, you can also ask your child to guess about the people with whom they're involved.

Ask the child to think of names for people you see around you. "Doesn't that older man over there with the long, stern face look like his name ought to be 'Horace'? Now what about the young woman with the outrageous hat in the far corner—what's a good name for her? And the plump woman in the flowery dress to her left . . . what do you think she looks like her name ought to be?"

# Alphabet Travels

2 or more players

In this game, players take turns naming the following things, all starting with the same letter:

- a name
- a destination
- an object
- an activity

The first player starts with the letter "A." He might say, for example, "My name is Adam, I'm going to Alaska, I'm packing an apple and I'm going to alphabetize."

If the first player gets through "A" successfully, he continues with the letter "B," giving answers in the same manner. The sentences don't have to make sense, as long as the right words are in the right places, starting with the right letters.

A player's turn ends when he makes a mistake or hesitates between letters. When this happen, the next player's turn begins. When the turn comes around to the first player again, he will pick up at the letter at which he left off on his previous turn. For example, if he made a mistake on the letter "F," he will now continue with the letter "G." The first person to complete the sequence with the letter "Z" wins the game.

## Variations

If there are more than two players, continue playing to determine second, third and fourth places, until all but one player is left.

With younger children, you may not want to include the letter "Q" and the letters after "T," all of which are harder. Instead, you can skip "Q" and end the game with "T."

# Buried Words

2 or more players
*Materials needed: Pen and old magazines*

Two or more children play this game together—as a challenge, not a competition.

Give each child an old magazine and ask her to choose an article. The object is for them to search for "buried words" within the sentences. For example, ask the children, "Can you find two buried animals? Here are examples of "buried words":

Thi**s nail** is in deep.

I **do g**ood things every day.

Give the children about two or three minutes to find the buried words. When the time is up, each child gives her article to the player on her left, who has to try to find buried words she missed.

# You Said A No-No

2 to 4 players
*Materials needed: Pen and paper, watch with a second hand*

Two players play in each round—one player is the "Wordmaster" and the other is "It." To begin, the Wordmaster writes down a word (other than "a," "an," "the," "you," "I" and "we"), making sure that no one sees it.

During the course of one minute, the Wordmaster asks It questions designed to make him use the secret word. For example, if the secret word is "school," the Wordmaster may ask, "What did you do today?" to try and get It to say, "I went to school."

If It uses the secret word within the minute, the Wordmaster says, "You're out! You said the secret word." He then shows It the paper with the secret word on it. However, if It avoids saying the secret word for the full minute, he wins.

Another way for It to win is to guess what the secret word is. He has three chances per round to do this. If he thinks he knows what the word is, he may say, "The Word is ____ ." If he's right, the round is over, and he wins.

In a two-player game, after the minute is up (or sooner if the round is over), the two players trade places. If three players are playing, the former It rotates out, the former Wordmaster becomes It, and the player who wasn't in the last round becomes the Wordmaster. With four players, the two who played last sit by and watch the other two play.

There are no cumulative points; each round is self-contained. But to make the game more fun, everyone should have a turn at being both It and Wordmaster.

# Sentences

2 or more players
*Materials needed: Pen and paper, watch with a second hand*

Before beginning this game, the players must decide two things: how many rounds they're going to play and who's going to be the first Wordmaster. (There is no particular advantage to being the first.) For example, if there are three players and they agree to play one round, each player will be Wordmaster once.

The Wordmaster thinks of a word that has four to six letters and says it aloud (for example, TRAVEL). All three players have two minutes to write as many sentences as they can that are comprised of words beginning (in order) with the letters "T - R - A - V - E - L." The sentences must make some kind of sense. Some examples may be: "Try

Relaxing And Visit East London," "Truly Reasonable Animals View Eating Lightly" and "Toys Really Are Very Exciting Lately." (Assign someone to keep an eye on a watch or clock and call, "Time" when two minutes are up.)

At the end of the two minutes, each player reads her sentences aloud. The other players verify the sentences to ensure that they make sense and start with the correct letters. Each player gets a point for each correct sentence she has. At the end of the game, add up the points. The player with the most points wins.

### Variation

To play noncompetitively, the players can think of sentences and say them out loud, without writing them down. This doesn't have to be timed.

# I Love My Love

2 or more players

This game is most fun when played as a silly game. It works better with younger children, who may not yet be able to remember long strings of words. The first player begins by saying, "I love my love because he's (or she's) ____," and fills in the blank with an adjective beginning with the letter "A" (for example, antsy, angelic, antiquated or agile). The adjective does not have to be a good rationale for romance, but it does have to start with "A."

The second player says, "I love my love because she's (or he's) ____," and fills in the blank with an adjective beginning with the letter "B." The third player (or the first player in a two-player game) repeats the formula, filling in the blank with an adjective that begins with the letter "C."

The game continues until the players have gone through the alphabet. However, unlike I'm Going Shopping (page 42), players do not repeat the previous players' contributions before adding their own. They are only required to remember what letter of the alphabet they have reached.

(page 42)

## Variations

If desired, you can play this game competitively. Whenever a player hesitates before answering or is unable to remember the letter he is on, he is out of the game.

# The Thirteenth Day Of Christmas

2 or more players

In this holiday memory game, one player begins by saying, "On the thirteenth day of Christmas, I returned to the store one ____," filling in the blank with any item (the sillier the better!). The item does not have to be from the "olden days," like the "maids a-milking" or "geese a-laying" featured in the popular song. The game is more fun if the players are very descriptive (for example, one moustache-less walrus or one round-trip ticket to the moon).

The second player repeats, "On the thirteenth day of Christmas, I returned to the store two ____ (filling in the blank with an item) and one ____ (repeating the first player's item)." The next player then repeats the phrase, adding a "three" to the configuration.

Play continues until a player forgets one of the items. That player leaves the game and the game continues until one player is left.

# Twenty Questions

2 or more players

Is it animal, vegetable or mineral? That's all the information the players will have in advance about the object to be identified in this traditional game.

Choose one player to be the leader. The leader thinks of a thing and gives the other players one clue about its identity: animal, vegetable or mineral. The other players must determine what the thing is by asking the leader twenty yes-or-no questions.

If there are more than two players, they take turns asking questions about the object or guessing what it is. If one player makes a wrong guess, it does not count as one of the group's twenty questions, but that player is out of the game. The remaining players continue guessing until they have asked all twenty questions or someone makes an accurate guess.

If no one guesses what the object is within twenty questions, the leader wins that round.

For a simpler game that is better suited to younger kids, see "I'm Thinking of Something" (page 66).

# Counting Challenge

2 or more players

Can your child count by twos (two, four, six, eight, ten, twelve)? Easy, you say? Well, then, what about counting by threes? That's a little harder.

Challenge the players to count by threes—and to keep going! Beyond 36, beyond 99, and so on. If that's too easy, challenge the player to count by fours, fives, sixes and higher.

The children will enjoy the challenge, and it is a fun way to pass time without fidgeting. They'll never even know they're getting some math practice!

# Ten To Get The Word

2 players
*Materials needed: Pen and paper*

Two players match wits in this word game. One player is "It" and the other player thinks of a secret four-letter word (it cannot be a person's name). The other player writes down any two of the four letters and draws dashes for the two missing letters. It can ask ten questions to guess the secret word. The ten questions can be letter guesses or other questions, such as "Is it a noun?" or "Is it a color name?" "Is there an 'A'?" and so on, until she guesses the word or until she asks ten questions.

The two players trade places and continue the game.

# Fortunately*

2 or more players

This game has no winners or losers and no formal ending.

The first player begins by stating an unfortunate circumstance in one sentence. For example, "The dog ate my homework Monday night." The second player chimes in with, "Fortunately . . . " For example, "Fortunately, it was early and I had time to do it again." The next player follows up with, "Unfortunately . . . " For example, "Unfortunately, my pen ran out of ink."

The game continues, with players rotating "fortunately" and "unfortunately." For example, the

---

* Apologies to Remy Charlip and his book *Fortunately* (Four Winds Press)

next player says, "Fortunately, I found my mom's lipstick and wrote with that." The next player says, "Unfortunately the teacher wouldn't accept home-work written in lipstick."

It goes on and on until the story comes to a dead end, a logical conclusion or everyone just gets tired of playing.

# Name That Tune

2 or more players

Can your children recognize a tune by its first three notes—hummed, no words?

Choose one player to go first. The first player thinks of a song and hums three notes. Starting with the player on her right, each player gets a chance to try and name the tune, if he can. If no one can name the song, the first player hums the first four notes. If everyone still strikes out, she hums the first five. When a player correctly guesses the song, it is his turn to think up a song for the others to guess.

## Variations

If you are playing with only one child, present it as a challenge rather than a competition. Hum the notes of songs that she knows and see how many notes of each song it takes for her to recognize the tune. If desired, the child can challenge you too. Can you name that tune?

# Don't Laugh At My Problems

2 or more players

Can you keep a smile off your face when someone's trying to make you laugh? That's the challenge in this game.

Pick one person to be the "emcee." The goal of the emcee is to make one of the other players laugh (or at least grin). The emcee poses a problem to each player in turn, such as, "My ostrich is molting," or "My uncle died and left me ten million dollars—provided I give a good home to his 467 pet ferrets." The other players have to keep a straight face while listening to the emcee's problems and giving ostensibly serious solutions.

Solutions to the two sample problems above might be: "You should go into the feather pillow business," and "Maybe you could breed the ferrets, sell the baby ferrets, and make another million dollars."

Play continues until a player cracks a grin. That player becomes the emcee and another round is started.

Variations

When there are only two players, they can take turns trying to crack up each other, with the winner being the one who holds out the longest.

# Alphabet Stories

2 or more players

This activity is similar to Progressive Stories (page 25); however, Alphabet Stories tend to be sillier and have a more limiting set of rules. Specifically, each player contributes one sentence at a time to the story. The first word of each sentence must begin with the letter that follows the letter that started the sentence preceding it. (It does not have to be a sensible sentence.)

One player begins the story with a sentence that begins with any letter. For example, "'Do you allow ostriches on this beach?' the hippo asked the lifeguard." Since the first player's sentence started with the letter "D," the next player's sentence must begin with the letter "E." He might say, for example, "'Everyone knows ostriches are only allowed at

Starfish Cove,' the lifeguard answered." The next player must now begin her sentence with the letter "F." For example, "'Forgive me, but which way is Starfish Cove?' the hippo asked."

The story progresses in this manner, all the way through the letter "Z" and back around to the letter "A," until you get back to the last letter that hasn't been used—in this case "C" (because the first sentence of the story started with a "D").

Of course, if everyone's having a great time, there's no reason to stop!

# Three-At-A-Time Stories

2 or more players

This activity shares a common principle with Progressive Stories (page 25), but the rules are different: Each person contributes only three words at a time to a story. Think it sounds easy? Think again!

The first player leads off with three words and stops. For example, "A boy named . . . " The second player gives the next three words and stops. He might add, "Mark, who wanted . . . " The next player adds three more words (for example, "to be a . . . "), and the game continues.

Unlike Progressive Stories, the players won't leave the protagonist in the middle of a cliffhanger; they'll leave him in the middle of a sentence!

The players should try to add their bits quickly, without much thought—it's funnier that way.

# Mystery Guest

4 or more players

One player plays the part of a TV talk show host while another person plays the mystery guest: a famous person who can be alive, dead or even fictional, and whose identity is not revealed until another player guesses it.

The host introduces the mystery guest with the usual flourish, and then begins to ask questions designed to elicit his identity. The guest may answer evasively if he wishes, but never dishonestly. For example, if the "mystery guest" is acting like the President and the host asks, "Do you live in a large house?" the guest must answer yes. However, he doesn't have to volunteer that he lives in the White House.

As the interview proceeds, the other players try to guess the identity of the mystery guest. When someone guesses correctly, the round is over.

To begin another round, two of the audience members can assume the roles of Host and Mystery Guest.

## Variations

If you like this game but only have two players, they can take turns being the host and the mystery guest, and the host can try to guess the guest's identity.

# Telephone Words

1 or more players
*Materials needed: Pen and paper*

Another activity to keep young minds occupied is to figure out what words they can spell using their telephone number. Each numeral on a telephone keypad has three letters assigned to it (except one and zero), so this activity takes a little longer than you might think.

You will be amazed at how many phone numbers equate to words, however silly the words might be. (For example, my phone number is WOW-A LOG—I think that qualifies as pretty silly!) The players can also use word/number combinations. For example, 253-GOES or WRONG-12.

# Words In Words

1 or more players
*Materials needed: Pen and paper, possibly a watch with a
second hand*

This is a good solitaire game, although several children can play.

Give each player a piece of paper and a pen and tell them a long word. The players try to make as many words as they can from the letters in the larger word.

For example, if the word is "intermediate," some of the smaller words may be: MEDIATE, MEDIA, ATE, DIET, TIDE, TIED, EDIT, TERM, INTER, MEDITATE, DIME, MIDI, MATE, RATE, MAT, RAT, MEAT, TEAM, TEAR, TARE, TAME, MEET, TRAM, TRADE, RANT, EMIT, TRIM, DARE, DEAR, DEER, READ, MINT, MIND, TRAIN, RAIN, DETER and DETERMINE.

You can give the players a fixed amount of time (for example, three or five minutes) or they can take as long as they need. The children can compete to see who can find the most words, or they can each try to do her best without competing.

Because the players do not need to know the meaning of the longer word to find the smaller words, you can pick a long word that is unknown to the children. Also, because this works so well as a solitaire game, it's perfect for only children!

# Rebuses

1 or more players
*Materials needed: Pen and paper*

The concept of rebuses and similar puzzles is that pictures, letters or numerals can be used to stand for syllables or entire words. A picture of a bee or the letter "B" can stand for "be," for example. A picture of a hand, followed by a "+" symbol and a lower case "y" is "handy." Pictures of an eye, a can, a fly, a lower case "a," and a plane spells: "I can fly a plane."

Explain the concept to your children and challenge them to dream up their own rebuses. They can work together or on their own. They can challenge each other to read each other's rebuses when they finish. If you only have one child, let him devise the rebuses for you to translate.

# I Got A Letter

3 or more players
*Materials needed: Pen and paper*

Give each player a piece of paper and a pen. Each player writes a brief letter (two or three sentences or a paragraph) to himself in the voice of a famous person, real or fictional, living or dead. The letter should contain clues to the writer's identity, without stating it outright.

Here are two examples of the kind of letter a player might write:

"Dear Susie,

How are you? I am fine, but yesterday while crossing the river, I stood up in the boat and nearly fell out. Army food is bad and hard to eat with my wooden teeth. I cannot tell a lie, so I have to admit that I would like to be president of the country some day if we win the war."

(answer: George Washington)

"Dear Evan,

I am w'iting to see if you can help me twap that wascally wabbit. I have twied all kinds of twaps, offered him cawwots and done evewything I can think of, but I cannot catch him. Ohh, he gets me so exaspewated. I have just twied to catch him again, but I failed. That is all my news. What's new with you? As he might say, 'What's up with you, Doc?'"

(answer: Elmer Fudd)

One at a time, each player reads her letter aloud, while the others listen. The first player to identify the alleged writer of the letter shouts out the person's name. If she is right, she gets a point. If she is wrong, though, she loses a point and cannot guess again during this letter. In that case, the player reading the letter continues reading, until someone else guesses correctly. (If no one can guess the identity, no points are awarded.)

The players continue to read their letters aloud. When all of the players have finished reading their letters, the player with the most points is declared the winner.

# Secret Letter

3 or more players
*Materials needed: Pen and paper*

The object of this game is for players to guess a secret letter and avoid scoring points.

Choose one person to be the leader for the first round. The leader writes any letter of the alphabet on a piece of paper, then asks the first player a question designed to elicit a one-word answer, such as "What is your favorite season?" Yes-or-no questions are invalid.

If the first player's one-word answer contains the secret letter, she gets a point. If she doesn't get a point, the leader asks the second player a different question. If, however, the first player gets a point, the second player has one chance to guess what the secret letter is.

If the second player guesses the secret letter correctly, the round is over and she becomes leader for the next round. If she doesn't guess the secret letter, she must answer a question. If she answers with a word that contains the secret letter, she gets a point. The next player gets to try and guess the secret letter. When a player correctly guesses the secret letter, the leader shows everyone the piece of paper with the letter on it.

A player who gets three points is out of the game. If all the players get three points before anyone guesses the secret letter, the leader remains for the next round.

# Letters By Number

3 or more players
*Materials needed: Pen and paper*

To play this game, children must be very familiar with the alphabet.

Choose one player to be the leader. Before the game starts, the leader writes the letters of the alphabet on a piece of paper, and the numbers 1-26 below the corresponding letters (for example, 1 below A, 2 below B, 3 below C and so on).

The leader calls out a letter (for example, "K"). The other players then scramble to figure out what number corresponds to K—counting on their fingers or just figuring in their heads. The first player to call out, "Eleven!" wins a point. Anyone who calls out an incorrect number loses a point.

You can play either to a predetermined score or for a predetermined length of time. If you play for a predetermined score, the first player to get 25 points (or another number) is the winner. If you play by time, the person who is ahead after 15 minutes (or another time limit) is the winner.

## Variations

Reverse the procedure by having the leader call out a number and the other players providing the corresponding letter. (For example, if the leader calls, "Five," the winning answer would be "E.") You can play a round of letters-by-number followed by a round of numbers-by-letter, or the leader can mix the two by sometimes calling out a number, and sometimes calling out a letter.

# Insta-Messages

2 or more players
*Materials needed: Pens and paper*

Each player takes turns suggesting a random letter until there are ten letters. As the players suggest letters, each player writes the letters on a piece of paper. When there are ten letters, each player writes a ten-word message using each of the ten letters as the initial letters of each word. For example, if the letters are: C, K, W, K, G, H, F, Y, N, and I, a possible message is: CROSSED KANGAROO WITH KITTEN. GOT HOPPING FURBALL. YOU NAME IT.

The sentences have to make sense, but they don't have to be sensible. Good grammar is not important either.

# Word Golf

1 or more players
*Materials needed: Pen and paper*

Children can play this game as a solo challenge or competitively. Ask your child or children how many "strokes" it would take him to change one word into another. The rules are: you can only change one letter at a time, and you can't transpose letters. As with real golf, the lower the score, the better.

For example, change STAR to MOON. Here is one solution:

STAR

SEAR

BEAR

BEAN

MEAN

MOAN

MOON

Six "strokes"—can your child do better than that?

How about changing SLOW to FAST? One possibility is:

SLOW
SLOT
SLAT
SEAT
FEAT
FEST
FAST

Again, six strokes. What's your child's score?

Since Word Golf is a great solitaire game, one player can play it or several players can work independently. If several children are playing, you can give them the same two words and challenge them to see how many "strokes" it takes them to complete the conversion. But it doesn't have to be a competitive challenge.

# Secret Languages: Pig Latin

2 or more players

If your children are young, they may not yet know how to speak Pig Latin. Do you have a long stretch of time to fill on a plane ride or another drawn-out situation? Here's a time-filler that can be stretched out quite a bit: Teach the children how to speak Pig Latin, and encourage them to practice it with each other (or, if you've only got one child, with you).

For those of you who are rusty on this language for which no school gives language credit, here's a brief refresher course: Chop off the initial consonant sound (both letters, if it's a combination sound, such as "sh," "th," or "st") of each word and tack it on to the end, then add "ay" after it. (For example, "happy" becomes "appy-hay.") If the word starts with a vowel, add "way" to the end.

(For example, "I'm" becomes "I'm-way.")

That's all there is to it! Now, translate the following sentence into Pig Latin:

"I'm happy to have learned to speak Pig Latin." Answer: "I'm-way appy-hay oo-tay ave-hay earned-lay oo-tay eak-spay ig-Pay atin-Lay." Got it? Now teach it to your children and watch them have a ball practicing!

# Secret Languages: Op

2 or more players
*Materials needed: None, or possibly pen and paper*

Pig Latin (page 117) has been a favorite with children for generations. However, there are other "secret languages" as well. Here is another one that can bring hours of fun:

Teach your children "Op." In this secret language, the children insert the syllable "op" after every syllable. For example:

*Probably* becomes, "prob-op-ab-op-ly-op."

*Looks like rain* becomes, "Looks-op like-op rain-op."

# Secret Languages: Gibberish

2 or more players

A more challenging language than "Op" (page 119) is "Gibberish." It is much easier to speak than it is to explain. So before you decide not to try it, remember that it sounds harder than it is.

In between every syllable of a word, insert the two-syllable combination, "d-[vowel] g-[vowel]," pairing each of these inserted syllables with the vowel from the syllable they follow. (This sounds much more complicated than it is!) For example:

*What* becomes: "Wha-da-ga-t."

*Cool!* becomes: "Coo-doo-goo-l!"

*What do you know?* becomes: "Wha-da-ga-t doo-doo-goo yoo-doo-goo kno-do-go-w?"

*Hermeneutics* becomes: "Her-der-ger-me-de-ge-neu-du-gu-ti-di-gi-cs."

This is easier to hear than to write. Say the above words and phrases aloud; you and your children will get the hang of it pretty quickly. You'll know you're speaking Gibberish fluently when you sound like you're speaking normally while trying to drink a glass of water!

## Variations

Encourage the children to invent their own languages. As you can see, all they need to make a new language is one or two simple rules! They may want to write down the rules for the language they've invented. Or they may want to avoid doing so, to keep their secret language more of a secret.

# Forbidden Letters

2 or more players

Choose one person to be the leader. The leader faces
the player on her left, names a letter of the alphabet and asks that player a question. The player must
answer the leader's question with a sentence containing at least six words, but none of the words
can have the forbidden letter named by the leader.
The player's reply must be responsive to the leader's
question, but it does not need to be truthful.

For example, the leader says to the player on
her left, "R. What's your greatest ambition?" The
player cannot answer, "To be the state's champion
fly fisherman," because the sentence contains the
letter "R." Instead, the player might answer, "I
want to win a million bucks," or "I want to live to
see an elephant fly." These answers may have noth-

ing to do with reality, but they answer the question, have at least six words, and do not contain the letter "R."

If the responding player is successful, he becomes the leader and turns to the player on his left, gives a letter, and asks the player a question. For example, "L. What do you want to do on your Christmas vacation?"

To make the game more difficult, especially with older players, you can impose a five-second time limit for players to respond to questions.

You can play this as a win/lose game or just for fun. If you are playing for fun, there are no points, no elimination and no winners. Play until you're tired of it, or you arrive at Grandma's. If you play this game competitively, eliminate players who err, then the winner is the last player left.

To keep everyone in the game and active, you can award points for each correct answer. This way, players who err stay in the game—they just don't get any points in the rounds in which they give unacceptable answers. At the end of the game, the player with the most points wins.

# Questions

2 or more players

This game is deceptively simple—the players must respond to each other's questions by asking other questions.

Play starts with one player asking a question. The player can ask almost any question he desires, such as, "What do you want for lunch?"

The next player has to respond without breaking the following rules:

1. You must answer with a question.

2. You cannot hesitate.

3. The question must somehow respond to the previous question.

For instance, a valid answer to, "What do you want for lunch?" might be, "Is there any tuna in the house?"

The next player responds likewise: "Since when do you like tuna?"

The questions fly until a player breaks one of the above rules. The player leaves the game, and play continues with the remaining players. Play ends when all but one have been eliminated.

# Spelling Bee/Knowledge Bee

2 or more players

Challenge your children to show off their spelling skills!

In turn, give each player a word to spell. If a player misses, she is out of the game. The winner is the last one in the game.

## Variations

If you find that the standard rules cause the game to be over too quickly, allow players to misspell three words before they are out. Or, set a limit on the number of rounds. For example, decree that the bee will consist of three (or another number) rounds.

If the players' ages are far apart, give each child age-appropriate words to spell.

# Backward Spelldown

3 or more players

Challenge your children to spell words backward. In turn, give each player a moderately long word to spell (in accordance with her spelling ability), and then listen as she attempts to spell it from back to front. As the players continue to spell words correctly, give them longer and more complicated words.

This game can be challenging. Therefore, it is best to play it non-competitively so that it's fun for everybody.

# Geography

2 or more players

Geography is a subject that many children enjoy. They can have fun while learning the names of many places around the world.

Choose one player to start. She names any place in the world, such as "Chicago," "Rio de Janeiro," "the Indian Ocean," "Antarctica" or "France."

The second player then names a place that begins with the last letter of the place the previous player named. For example, if the first player says, "Maryland," which ends with a "D," the second player might say, "Durham." The next player must name a place that begins with the letter "M," such as "Mexico." That player could not name "Maryland" again because a place cannot be repeated.

If a player is unable to supply an appropriate geographical name on his turn, he drops out of the game. The last player left is the winner.

# 9

# Buzz

2 or more players

Players choose a number between two and nine to be the "Buzz Number." The players take turns counting out loud by ones, starting at the number one. The rule is that they can never say any number containing the buzz number, nor can they say any numbers that are multiples of it. Instead, they say, "Buzz!"

For example, the players might choose seven to be the buzz number. The players take turns counting. The first player leads off, saying, "One." The second player says, "Two." The third player says, "Three." This continues until a player gets to a buzz number (such as seven, fourteen, seventeen and so on) and he says, "Buzz!"

A player is out of the game if he fails to say, "Buzz" at the appropriate time or if he says it on a number that doesn't contain the buzz number or isn't a multiple of it. In addition, any player who says a number or "Buzz" out of turn is also out. The last player remaining is the winner.

# 10

# Fizz-Buzz

2 or more players

Fizz-Buzz is a more involved version of "Buzz" (page 131). Players choose one number to be the buzz number, and treat it the same as in "Buzz": they take turns counting by one, substituting every number that contains the buzz number or is a multiple of the buzz number with "Buzz."

Here is the twist: players also choose a second number to be the "Fizz Number." The players treat the fizz number the same way as the buzz number, substituting "Fizz" for the number and multiples of the number.

For the final twist: if a number contains both the fizz number and the buzz number (or is a multiple of both), players will say, "FIZZ-BUZZ!" (Or, "BUZZ-FIZZ," depending on the player's mood!).

For example, If seven is the buzz number and five is the fizz number, play would sound like this: "One, two, three, four, Fizz!, six, Buzz!, eight, nine, Fizz!, eleven, twelve, thirteen, Buzz!, Fizz!, sixteen, Buzz!, eighteen, nineteen, Fizz!, Buzz!, twenty-two, . . . " The last player remaining is the winner.

# About the Author

Cynthia MacGregor is the author of *Raising a Creative Child*, *365 After-School Activities* and *Totally Terrific Family Games*. She lives in Lantana, Florida.